Dog friendly
Pub Walks
Cotswolds

Wet Nose
Publishing Ltd

www.countrysidedogwalks.co.uk

First published in September 2016 by **Wet Nose Publishing Ltd**
All enquiries regarding sales telephone: 01824 704398
email cdw@wetnosepublishing.co.uk
www.countrysidedogwalks.co.uk
ISBN 978-0-9931923-5-7

"Tips are low this week"

"What do you mean the beer tastes ruff?
Get out of my pub you filthy animal....you're barked!"

Contents

Introduction 1

1. Broadway - Crown & Trumpet Inn (Medium) 9

2. Chipping Campden - Lygon Arms (Medium) 15

3. Snowshill - Snowshill Arms (Medium) 21

4. Cleeve Common - Rising Sun Hotel (Med/Chall) 25

5. The Windrush - Black Horse Inn (Medium) 31

6. Slaughters - Slaughters Inn (Easy) 39

7. Finstock - Plough Inn (Easy) 43

8. Birdlip - The Royal George Hotel (Medium) 47

9. Buckholt Wood - The Blackhorse Inn (Medium) 51

10. Miserden - Carpenter's Arms (Medium) 57

11. Uley Bury - The Old Crown Inn (Challenging) 61

12. Tindale Monument - The Black Horse (Med/Chall) 65

13. Swineford - The Swan (Easy) 69

14. River Avon - The Boathouse (Easy) 75

15. Combe Hay - The Wheatsheaf (Challenging) 79

16. Avoncliff - Cross Guns (Medium) 85

Introduction

The walks included in this book are all designed so that you and your wet nosed friend have a really enjoyable time. Where there are stiles, they are specially designed with lift gates for dogs. At a quick glance there is information at the beginning of each walk to tell you what to expect and what you may need to take with you. The descriptive guides will also warn of any roads ahead or areas of livestock so that you can get your dog on the lead well in advance.

Dogs just love to explore new places. They really enjoy the new smells and carry themselves a little higher with the added excitement. Going to new places gets you and your dog out and about, meeting new people and their dogs. It is important to socialise dogs, as they will be more likely to act in a friendly manner towards other dogs, as they gain confidence.

The stunning pictures in this book are just a taster of what you can see along the way. Many of the walks have fantastic views and scenery. Some of the walks are wooded, offering shade on those hot summer days.

The walks are graded Easy, Medium and Challenging. They are all around one to three hours long, depending on your and your dog's pace. You may start

with the easy ones and work up to the challenging walks depending on your and your dog's fitness. Different dog breeds and dog age must be taken into account when you decide which walks to do.

Different breeds of dog have different levels of fitness. For example, bulldogs can only do short walks whereas a border collie or a springer spaniel are extremely energetic and difficult to tire out. It is recommended that you do some research on the breed of dog that you own to get to know what sort of exercise that they require.

You may have a walk that you are happy doing with your dog every day, but this book will show you new areas to explore with a change of scenery and a chance to meet new people and their dogs. Dogs love new places to visit and you will see the change in them as they explore the new surroundings, taking in the new smells with delight. You will fulfil both your life and your dog's just by trying somewhere new.

Some of the walks include bridleways, so you may encounter horses and cyclists. It is important to put your dog on a lead if you see horses approach. It is always helpful to say hello to the riders as they near so that the horse realises that you are not a threat.

Ground Nesting Birds

Watch out for vulnerable ground nesting birds from March to the end of July. Dogs that stray off the main paths may disturb birds and chicks, possibly killing them or breaking eggs. Species to look out for are Skylarks, Meadow pipits, Curlew, Red and Black grouse, Snipe and Pheasants.

Some if not all of these birds are declining in numbers, due partly to their vulnerability when nesting. Dogs are a threat to them, even if treading on them unintentionally. Some other threats are foxes, badgers, stoats, weasels, birds of prey and crows.

Please help to protect these birds during the nesting season by keeping your dog on the paths when walking in open areas such as grassland, moors, heathland and scrub.

Rivers

Some dogs love water and will think nothing of plunging into the river. With the extreme weather conditions over the last few years, a river that may be safe for your dog to swim in can change in a matter of hours, to become a swollen torrent that could wash your dog away.

Please be careful when near rivers if there have been heavy periods of rain or if they look swollen or fast flowing. It is best to put your dogs on the lead, until you have assessed the situation.

Livestock

If you find that you need to cross a field with cattle or horses and they seem interested in you or your dog it is recommended within the Countryside Code to let your dog off the lead. Never try to get between livestock and your dog. Your dog will get out of a situation a lot more easily with speed than you can. It is usually only cattle with young calves that are a threat, or young heifers or bullocks that tend to get a little inquisitive. They will usually stop when they get close to you or your dog.

Most horses will come over for a fuss but a small proportion do have a problem with dogs. They may see them as a threat and will act to defend the herd. Horses that are out with a rider are completely different as they are not defending the herd, and as long as you keep a safe distance there should not be a problem.

Sheep are not a danger to you, but your dog can be a danger to them. Where sheep are grazing it is vital that you have your dog on a lead or under very close control. You will know your dog, but if you are unsure it is better to play safe and keep your dog on a lead. It is important always to have your dog on a lead when around lambs. Lambs have a higher pitched bleat and can be the size of a cat, and your dog may act differently amongst them.

Pub Etiquette

All the pubs featured in this book welcome you and your dog, so you can relax part way around or at the end of a good walk. Dogs must be kept on a lead whilst inside the pub and we would ask that you consider other people. For instance, please don't allow your dog to lie down in the doorways or in thoroughfares. In wet weather, avoid your dog shaking his coat where he may spray mud onto people, which is not very pleasant, especially if they are eating. Remember, not all people like dogs, and some people may be allergic to them, or even frightened of them. If you consider this before going in it will help towards ensuring that the pub that you are visiting stays dog-friendly. **Please Note:** we recommend you telephone in advance to check opening times and to book in advance for meals.

Does your dog fetch a stick?

Most dogs love sticks and will pick them up without any encouragement from their owners. Vets and dog trainers recommend that you should not throw sticks for dogs. They can cause nasty injuries, sometimes fatal as the stick can pierce the throat, or rebound off the ground and cause harm to your dog.

Ticks

If you have been walking in areas where sheep graze you should check your dog for ticks. They must be removed as soon as possible. It is best to use tick tweezers, which are specially designed to remove the head and leg parts of the tick. Ticks can carry diseases and the longer they remain latched on to your dog the more the chance of spreading infections.

Dogs and Alcohol

Please note: alcohol is poisonous to dogs!

Throughout this book there are jokes about dogs drinking alcohol, this is intended as humour by humanising dogs in funny situations. Any dog pictured drinking beer is only supping alcohol-free drinks and it must be stressed that dogs should never be given alcohol.

Please clean up after your dog

Always be prepared, having dog bags with you at all times. Once you have cleaned up after your dog, please keep the bag, until you see a bin. If there are no bins provided, then take it away with you to a roadside bin. Dog bags that are discarded on the paths or in the bushes are unpleasant, unsightly and will not degrade.

"Aaaah, a well earned pint at last!"

1. Broadway - Crown & Trumpet Inn

Tel: 01386 853202 Medium - 4 miles - 2hr 30min

This is a wonderful circular walk, where you will find the pub at the end when you have completed the walk. Follow on part of the Cotswold Way long distance route, which will pass across farmland on a path between fences for some of the way. You will go through Broadway Coppice Wood, and then continue on the edge of farmland. You will descend to the village of Buckland. From there you will ascend across farmland again, before returning on your outbound path. There is a short section on a quiet village road. There may be livestock in parts of the walk.

Please Note: There are some stiles, with small lift gates. Dogs larger than a Labrador won't fit through.

How to get there – From the M5 turn off at junction 9, and follow the signs for Evesham A46, and Tewkesbury A438. Continue on the A46 and follow signs for Evesham. Before you reach Evesham, turn right following the sign for Broadway, on Broadway Road. Pass a car park on your left, and at the end of the road turn left. Shortly after, on the main road turn right. Turn right again on to Church Street, following the sign for short stay car park until you reach it.

Grid Reference – SP 094373   **Postcode** – WR12 7AE

Parking – Short stay car park pay and display on Church Close, off Church Road

Facilities – There are toilets in the car park

You will need – Dog lead, dog bags and water for your dog

The Walk

1 From the car park, with your back to the entrance to the ladies toilet, continue straight ahead to the edge of the car park, where you will find a pedestrian entrance, marked with a footpath sign. Shortly after, on reaching another grass path turn right. Keep your dog on a lead, as there is a road ahead. Cross the road and continue straight ahead on the access track, which is sign posted for the Cotswold Way (CW) and West End Lane. You will pass cottages on your right, and on reaching the end of the track, keep your dog on a lead or under close control and go through the kissing gate on your left. There may be livestock in the field.

Continue straight ahead on the edge of the field. At the end of the field, cross a footbridge over a stream. Your dog can get water here. Go through the kissing gate and continue straight ahead, following the sign for the CW. At the end of the field you will reach a road. Put your dog on the lead; pass through the kissing gate and cross the road. Go through the small gate straight ahead, which is signed for the CW. Ascend between a hedgerow and a fence. Turn a series of bends and then pass through a kissing gate.

Keep your dog under close control or on a lead, as there may be livestock. Continue straight ahead on the edge of a field, beside the hedgerow on your right. Ascend gently to begin with, and then the ascent will become a little steeper. You will continue beside woodland on your right. You will soon enter the wood, which is known as Broadway Coppice.

On reaching another path, turn left and follow the waymarker signed for the CW. Soon after, ascend the steps and then go through a kissing gate. Keep your dog under close control or on a lead, as there may be livestock. Continue on the edge of the field, beside the hedgerow on your left, following the sign for CW. On reaching the end of the field, go through two kissing gates in close succession. Continue straight ahead.

On reaching the corner of the field, go through the small gate and continue straight ahead between fences and fields. Pass through a small gate and then turn right on the track, which is a byway. ❷ Descend between the fences, with fields beyond. You will pass a house on your right, and just after, pass a footpath on your left. You will see a pond on your left, and then pass a driveway to a house on your left. You will pass another house and then a footpath on your right.

Continue past houses on your left (Buckland Court). Just after, take the footpath on your left and ascend on the Winchcombe Way. ❸ Pass a drive on your left and continue straight ahead. Just after, take the steps on your right and then go through a kissing gate. Keep your dog under close control or on a lead. Continue straight ahead and ascend through a field, where there is no obvious path. As you continue you will see a waymarker. On reaching a stile cross it, using the lift gate for your dog. Continue on the obvious grass path, ascending steeply between newly planted trees. On reaching another stile at the end of the plantation, cross it and continue straight ahead through the middle of another field, keeping your dog under close control or on a lead. You will cross a stream, where your dog can get a drink.

Continue straight ahead, and on reaching the end of the field, cross another stile and then continue straight ahead ascending on the edge of a field, with a stock fence on your left. On reaching the end of the field cross another stile and continue between fences, through a copse of trees. On reaching another stile, cross it and turn left on a track. Keep your dog under close control or on a lead. Ignore a kissing gate on your right. Pass through a gate and continue between the stock fences.

At the end of the path, put your dog on a lead, go through the gate into a farmyard. ❹ Turn left when you reach the farm buildings and pass through another farm gate. Continue on the access track, keeping your dog under close control in case of traffic. You will eventually reach a familiar spot, near the wooden barn. Turn right beside the fingerpost, following the sign for CW. You will now retrace your steps, following the signs for the CW. After going through the wood, known as Broadway Coppice, descend on the familiar path and after going through the kissing gate put your dog on a lead, as there is a road ahead.

Cross the road and pass through the kissing gate opposite. Continue through the middle of the field, and head for the church in the distance. Cross the footbridge, where your dog can cool off in the stream. Continue straight ahead and on reaching the road, cross over and turn left. Pass the church on your right, cross the road, where you will then reach the pub on your right.

On leaving the pub turn left on the road, retrace your steps, and pass the church on your left, and then take the path on your left. Continue on the path, where you will turn left to enter back into the car park.

Slurp, slurp "Waste not, want not!"

2. Chipping Campden - Lygon Arms

Tel: 01386 840318   Medium - 3 miles - 2hr

Dover's Hill is a popular spot for visitors, where on a clear day you will have wonderful views. You will descend through farmland, and in some places you will be between fences. Walk through the picturesque village of Chipping Campden, and you will reach the pub at the halfway point. Retrace your steps through the village, and then take a different route back to the car park. There are some roads with pavements, and you will pass through fields, where livestock may be grazing.

How to get there – The car park is found on the outskirts of Chipping Campden. From Chipping Campden, follow the sign for Dover's Hill on Dyers Lane. Continue straight ahead at the cross roads, where you will find the car park shortly after on your right.

Grid Reference – SP 137395

Postcode – GL55 6UW

Parking – Free in the National Trust car park

Facilities – There are no facilities, except in the pub

You will need – Dog lead, dog bags and water for your dog

The Walk

❶ Go through the gate in the corner of the car park, beside the interpretation panel. Keep your dog under close control or on a lead, as there may be livestock. Continue straight ahead, towards the topograph, on the obvious worn path. On reaching the topograph, you will have fantastic views on a clear day. Turn right, and continue beside the steep slope on your left. Your views will soon be blocked because of the trees and scrub.

Continue on the obvious path until you reach a trig point (triangular concrete block) on your right. From the trig point, cross the field and then turn left. ❷ You will soon reach a kissing gate on your right. Go through the kissing gate and continue between stock fences and then hedgerows, with fields beyond. Descend gently, keeping your dog on a lead, as there is a road ahead.

On reaching the road, cross with care and then turn right on the grass verge for a short distance. Take the footpath on your left, which is signed Chipping Campden. Continue

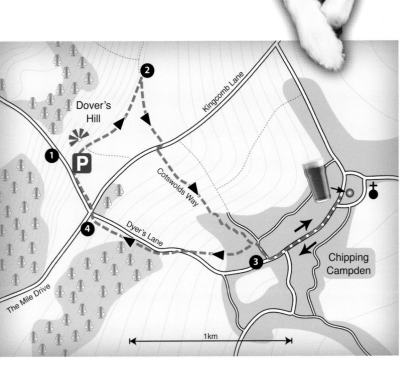

through the middle of a crop field, descending gently. Keep your dog on the path, to avoid any crop damage. On reaching the corner of the field, put your dog on a lead, or under close control and pass through the kissing gate. Descend and then pass through another kissing gate shortly after. Continue straight ahead, where you cross through another field. Head towards the kissing gate, which you will see as you continue to descend.

Pass through the kissing gate and continue between fields, beside the stock fence on your right. At the end of the field, go through the kissing gate and continue between gardens. You will reach a cul de sac. Descend, and on reaching a sharp left bend, take the footpath on your right. Cross a footbridge over a stream and continue beside the fence on your right. On reaching another road, turn right and continue around a sharp left bend.

Continue on the road, and cross the head of a cul de sac on your left. Take a footpath on your left and continue between garden fences. Continue on the access road. On reaching a road, turn right. At the end of the road, turn left. ❸ Pass St Catherine's Church on your left and continue through the village. Keep to your left and continue on a quiet narrow road. You will pass a parking area on your right, and then pass a war memorial. Just after, you will pass an arched building, which is the old market hall.

Continue along the main street for about another 100 yards. You will see the Lygon Arms on your right, on the opposite side of the road. You will find the bar after passing under the arch on the cobble path.

On leaving the pub turn left on the road and continue through the village. Cross the junction of Sheep Street on your left and continue on the main road. When you reach the church again on the opposite side of the road, cross

over. Turn right and continue to retrace your steps. Turn left on Birdcage Walk. Ignore the footpath on your right, signed for Dover's Hill and continue straight ahead between gardens. On reaching a road, cross over and continue straight ahead between the garden fences. On reaching a field go straight ahead, through an open gate and take the footpath which veers to your right, cutting diagonally across the crop field. Keep your dog under close control, as there is a road ahead.

On reaching the opposite side of the field, descend to the road. Cross over and then turn right on the grass verge. After about 100 yards cross a driveway and shortly after, veer left following the sign for the footpath. Keep your dog on a lead, or under close control, as the footpath continues beside the road, and there are gaps in the fence.

Ascend between the trees, with woodland on your left and a road on your right. As you continue past the woodland you will reach an open crop field. Put your dog on a lead as there is a road ahead. Continue on the edge of the field and ascend quite steeply. In the corner of the field, continue to the road beside a fingerpost. There are views on your left and behind you. ❹

Cross the road and continue straight ahead at the junction of another road. Go through a kissing gate on your right just after. Turn left and continue beside a hedgerow on the edge of a field. On reaching the corner of the field, go through three gates in close succession, and then turn right and enter back into the car park.

"I'm the owner of this place, so I'll sit wherever I choose!"

3. Snowshill - Snowshill Arms

Tel: 01386 852653   Medium - 2.3 miles - 1hr 30min

This is a delightful walk, where you will pass through farmland with mature parkland trees and woodland. There are views across beautiful hilly countryside. There are leafy quiet country roads, which lead to the delightful Snowshill village and the pub, which is close to the end of your walk. There are some ascents to climb and there may be livestock grazing on parts of the walk. There is a stream, where your dog can get a drink.

How to get there – From the M5 turn off at junction 9 and follow the signs for Evesham A46 and Tewkesbury A438. Continue on the A46 and follow signs for Evesham. Before you reach Evesham, turn right following the sign for Broadway, on Broadway Road. Pass a car park on your left, and at the end of the road turn left. Shortly after, on the main road turn right. Turn right again on to Church Street, following the sign for Snowshill. Continue on this road for about 2.5 miles, where you will reach the car park on your right, on the edge of the village.

Grid Reference – SP 096341   **Postcode** – WR12 7JU
Parking – Free in the car park on the outskirts of Snowshill village
Facilities – The are no facilities, except in the pub
You will need – Dog lead, dog bags

Dog Friendly Pub Walks - Cotswolds

The Walk

❶ From the car park, go through the small gate beyond the entrance. Continue through the overflow car park for Snowshill Manor. On reaching an entrance road turn right. After passing the entrance gate, take the kissing gate on your left, just before reaching the road.

Continue straight ahead, staying close to the field boundary on your right. There are views on your left and ahead of hilly countryside and woodland. There are mature ash trees in the field on your left. The path veers to your left and you will reach a kissing gate. Pass through the gate and continue straight ahead, but veer to your left.

Follow the worn grass path. You will see a large post ahead, and then in the distance a kissing gate. Continue past the post and then descend across the field, where you will reach the kissing gate. Pass through the gate and continue ahead and slightly to your left. Descend the sloping field, where you will soon reach a gate in the corner of the field.

Pass through the gate into woodland. There is a stream where your dog can get water on your left. Continue on the worn path through the wood. Ignore a path on your right and continue to

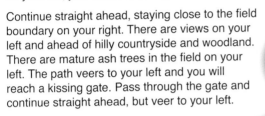

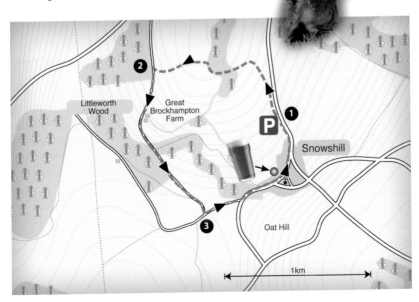

ascend. After about 100m ignore a gate straight ahead, and follow the path which bends sharply to your right. Walk beside the stock fence on your left. The path is narrow and has many tree roots.

You ascend on the edge of the woodland on a moderate slope. The path bends sharply to your left, where you leave the woodland. Continue straight ahead and cross the edge of a narrow section of field. Pass through a gate straight ahead and ascend once again. There is a stock fence on your left, and views on your left and right.

The gradient steepens as you approach the trees. Continue through the trees and pass through a metal kissing gate and turn left onto the track. ❷ Descend between the stock fence and fields. Pass some outbuildings on your right, and then houses on your left. Continue on the access road where you will have views on your left. Ignore a footpath on your left and begin to ascend.

As you continue you will see Snowshill village on your left, and the stunning countryside which surrounds it. Continue around a left bend in the road. ❸ Ignore a right turn and descend the quiet road, where you will reach Snowshill village. Continue on this road, where you will reach the pub on your left. On leaving the pub, continue on the road you were on, and you will then reach the car park on your left.

4. **Cleeve Common** - Rising Sun Hotel

Tel: 01242 676281   Med/Chall. - 4 miles - 2hr 30min

This superb circular walk has wonderful scenery, which has been formed from a vast disused quarry. The quarry has been reclaimed by nature and now has many small hills covered in grassland. There are spectacular views across most of the walk. There are beautiful wild flowers in the spring and summer. There is a pool half way around, where your dog can cool off. During nesting season you are asked to keep your dog on the paths to avoid disturbing ground nesting birds. There are sheep grazing on the common during the summer months. The pub is located near to the end of your walk.

How to get there – From Cheltenham, follow the signs for Prestbury, and then take the B4632, following the sign for Winchcombe. Where a grass island divides the middle of the road, turn right in the gap, which has a brown sign for Cleeve Hill Golf Course. Continue past the golf course entrance, where you will then reach the car park.

Grid Reference – SO 989270   **Postcode** – GL52 3PW

Parking – Free in the car park (note the times of car park closure)

Facilities – There are no facilities except at the pub

You will need – Dog lead, dog bags

The Walk

❶ From the car park, head back towards the entrance, and take the track on your right. You are now on part of the Cotswold Way long distance route. Continue on the track. Keep your dog under close control as you continue beside the golf course. There may also be sheep grazing. There is a stone wall and stock fence on your left to begin with. As you continue, the path descends and veers away from the stone wall. You will have views on your left and ahead.

You will pass a sheep pen on your left, and then reach a gate. Pass through the gate and continue to descend, now on a stone path between hedgerows. As you continue, ignore a footpath on your left and continue straight ahead. You will reach another farm gate straight ahead. Pass through it, and turn right on the second path and descend into the valley. **❷**

There are wonderful views ahead, which extend past the old quarried hills to the hills beyond. On reaching a waymarker ignore the path on your left and continue straight ahead, where you leave the Cotswold Way and continue on a level grass track. Continue on the main track, where you descend beside a stock fence and dilapidated stone wall on your left, and a row of mature beech trees. The track bends to your left. Continue on the main track, where a little further on it bends sharply to your left. Pass a footpath over a stile on your left and

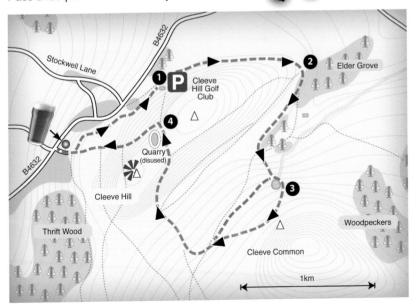

continue straight ahead on the main track. The landscape opens up, with views across the old quarry, which has created many hills.

Continue straight ahead on the main grass track, where you will reach 'The Wash Pool'. ❸ Your dogs can cool off here. You can choose from two paths here, one being elevated and the other in the valley. For the valley, turn right and continue on the main path, ignoring any paths which ascend (now skip the next two paragraphs).

If you wish to take the elevated path, pass the pool on your right (keep the concrete dam on your right), and take the path which ascends steeply on your right. You will reach a bench, where you can sit and enjoy the wonderful views, across the quarry and beyond. Continue on this path, as you walk along the fairly level ridge, with the valley below on your right.

Ignore any minor paths and stay on the ridge on the main path. As you continue you will pass amongst gorse and hawthorn. You will cross a minor track, nothing more than a sheep track, and continue amongst the gorse and hawthorn scrub. The path narrows and you continue straight ahead. You will descend gradually into the valley. As you continue you will see three aerial masts ahead. Continue between the gorse and hawthorn.

Just after you reach the bottom of the valley, both top and bottom paths meet. You will reach another grass track, in a slightly sloped open area. Veer to your right. You will then ascend out of the valley between the scrub. Where the path splits, take the path on your right. Ignore a path on your right and continue straight ahead. The path will veer to your right and you will be amongst amazing scenery, with fabulous views on your right across miles of countryside for as far as the eye can see. Continue on this path, amongst gorse and hawthorn.

Cross a grass track and then ascend where you will reach a gravel track. Turn right on this track where you will enjoy panoramic views. Continue on this surfaced track, which then descends towards a flag, where golf balls are played. Keep your dog under close control or on a lead, and beware of flying golf balls. Ascend again on the track, where you can enjoy views once again on your right. You will pass a golf course storage building on your left. There are stunning panoramic views, where you will see across Cleeve on your left,

as you begin to descend. As you continue you will see the golf house ahead. There is a large quarried hollow on your left. Take the narrow path on your left after you pass the hollow.

On reaching another surfaced track turn left. ❹ Pass the quarry hollow on your left and continue straight ahead, on the track marked Cotswold Way. There are fantastic views now on your right and then ahead. You will soon leave the Cotswold Way, as it veers to your left. Continue straight ahead and descend on the grass path. Cross a narrow path and continue to descend. Continue between banks, and ignore a path which veers to your left, as you reach a copse of mature trees.

Pass the copse of trees on your left and continue to descend. Keep your dog under close control or on a lead, as there is an access road ahead. On reaching the access road/track, put your dog on a lead and pass through the gate beside the cattle grid. Descend on the quiet road. On reaching a castellated house, turn right and enter into the pub car park. The bar is on your left. Don't enter the reception entrance, but enter the restaurant entrance. Descend the steps on your left, and follow the sign for Bar.

On leaving the pub, retrace your steps and pass through the gate beside the cattle grid. Turn left on the track, and keep your dog under close control, as you will continue on the access road for a short distance. There may also be sheep/cattle in the area. Where the track splits stay on your right. You are now free from traffic. Stay on this path and ascend past an isolated house on your left. Continue straight ahead, on the obvious path beside the old estate fence on your left. The fence veers sharply to your left. Continue straight ahead, and put your dog on a lead. There is a quarry face ahead, which has a sheer drop. There is a fence, but your dog can get on the wrong side of the fence at the beginning. Golf is also in play ahead.

You will reach the golf house as you pass the quarry. Keep your dog on a lead, or under close control and continue to a track, where there is a fingerpost on your right. Continue straight ahead on the track, where you will reach the car park on your left.

Dog Friendly Pub Walks - Cotswolds

5. The Windrush - The Black Horse Inn

Tel: 01451 850565   Medium - 9 miles - 3hr 30min

This linear walk begins in the picturesque village of Bourton-on-the-Water, and will follow beside the River Windrush for a good part of the walk. You pass through woodland, farmland and a quiet valley, before you reach the pub in the pretty village of Naunton, at the furthest point of the walk. There are two busy roads to cross, and you will be amongst sheep/cattle and possibly horses for parts of the walk. There is a low stone stile in Naunton village (about one and a half feet high) to cross.

How to get there – Bourton-on-the Water is located off the A429 between Cirencester and Shipston-on-Stour. Turn off the A429, and follow the sign for Bourton-on-the-Water at the traffic lights/pedestrian crossing where you will see the sign for coach and car park. Follow the signs and the car park is on your right.

Grid Reference – SP 169206

Postcode – GL54 2AA

Parking – Pay and display coach and car park (long stay)

You will need – Dog lead, dog bags

The Walk

❶ Start from the toilet block, near to the entrance. With the entrance to the toilets on your left, continue straight ahead. Turn left on reaching the ticket dispenser. Continue through the car park, where you will pass a kiosk on your right. Continue straight ahead on the footpath, leaving the car park. At the end of the path, turn right. Continue on a tarmac path. On reaching a road, cross over and continue straight ahead on another tarmac path. Pass some cottages on your left. At the end of the path, turn left and pass the church on your left.

On reaching the road, cross over and turn left, and continue through the village. Take the next road on your right, named Sherborne. Cross the bridge and continue on the road. **❷** As you reach a house in the middle of the road (fork), take the footpath on your right, which is signed Windrush Way. Continue between the buildings. At the end of the path, go through the kissing gate. Your dog can go off the lead here.

Continue on the path, with fields on your left and a narrow strip of grassland and the River Windrush on your right. Pass through a kissing gate and continue beside the river. Cross a footbridge and then put your dog on a lead. Continue on the path beside a hedgerow, now with the river on your left. On reaching the road, turn left. Continue on to the end of this road, where you will continue beside the river on your left.

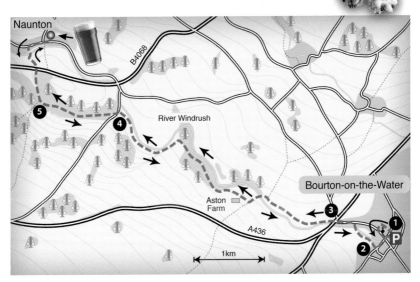

❸ On reaching the main road, cross with care and then take the bridleway on the opposite side, which is signed Windrush Way. Pass through a small gate, and continue between the fences. You will pass through a gate, where you enter into a field. Continue straight ahead, on the field edge, keeping your dog under close control as there may be livestock. At the end of the field, descend and pass a gate post. Continue on the well-worn path between trees.

A little further on you will reach a fork. Take the path on your right, marked with a blue arrow. Continue on the edge of the field, with trees on your left. Descend to the end of the field, and then continue to ascend between trees. Turn left, and descend onto a quiet road. Pass some cottages, and then cross a bridge over the river. After about 100m turn right following the sign for Windrush Way, and enter into a farm yard. Pass a farmhouse on your right, and continue through the farmyard. On reaching a concrete slab continue straight ahead, between farm buildings. Cross a field on the wide track.

At the end of the field continue through the wood, on a path which has many ascents and descents. There are some glades on your left, where there have been clearings in the woodland. As you leave the wood, continue straight ahead on the edge of a meadow. On reaching the corner of the field, go through the gate and veer to your left. Keep your dog under close control or on a lead, as there may be sheep grazing. Descend between trees and scrub. Continue to descend on the obvious path through the sloping grassland. As you reach level ground, continue beside the river on your right. Pass through several fields and gates, and keep your dog under close control or on a lead. Continue straight ahead through the fields on the obvious worn path, with the

river over on your right. Continue through another field, where you will see a house and farm buildings on the opposite side of the river. On reaching another gate, put your dog on a lead and go through the gate and turn left on the road. ❹

Ascend for about 40 metres. Just before you reach a metal gate on your right, turn right, following the Windrush Way sign post. Pass through a gate, keeping your dog under close control or on a lead, as there may be livestock. Veer to your left, and descend into a valley. Continue close to the telegraph line. At the end of the field, pass through the gate and continue straight ahead, through the middle of another narrow field. On reaching the end of the field, pass through another gate and continue straight ahead, where you are now on the edge of a sloped field, with trees on your right.

Go through another gate and turn right. ❺ Ascend through the field, where you will ascend out of the valley. Near the top of the slope, pass through a gate and continue on a track between the trees, with a stone wall on your right. Keep your dog under close control, as there is a golf course and a busy road ahead. Continue on the wide track through the golf course, which is screened by scrub and trees in places. Put your dog on a lead before reaching the end of the track. Cross the road, and continue straight ahead on the edge of a field, with a stock fence on your right. Descend between the hawthorns.

Leave the track where the fence on your right kinks to the right. Turn right, and descend between the trees, with a stock fence on your right and field beyond. Just before you reach a gate turn right. Pass through a small gate and continue straight ahead beside trees, with the river on your left. Pass through a kissing gate and continue beside the river on a narrow path, with a stone wall on your right. Keep your dog under close control, as there is a road ahead.

Put your dog on a lead as you reach a small stone stile. Cross over the stone and turn left on the access road. Cross a bridge and continue to the road. Turn right, and you will see the pub almost immediately on your left.

On leaving the pub turn right, and retrace your steps along the river. At the end of the path turn left, where you leave the river behind. Ascend on the edge of the field. Cross the road, and continue on the track across the golf course. Descend the sloping field on the obvious track. Continue through the valley, but remember after you pass through the 3rd gate to veer to your right, and ascend out of the valley. Go through the gate to reach the road and turn left. Descend, and on reaching level ground, take the familiar footpath on your right, following the Windrush Way and continue through the fields.

After you pass through three gates (not including the gate on the road) continue a little further and then ascend on the familiar path between the scrub. Go through the gate and continue beside the stock fence on the edge of the field. Continue through the wood, and then cross the field, where you will go back through the farmyard. Turn left onto the road. Cross the bridge and continue past the cottages. Ascend on the track and then turn right, following the Windrush Way. Ascend between the trees, and then beside a field. Continue through the wood, and then on the field edge. After going between the fences you will reach the main road, so put your dog on a lead in good time. Cross the road and continue straight ahead.

Just after reaching a house on your right, take the footpath on the right, following the sign for the Windrush Way. On reaching the end of the narrow grass area, put your dog on a lead and pass through a kissing gate. On reaching the road, turn left. At the end of the road, cross over and continue straight ahead on the residential road. Shortly after turn right, following the sign for car park. Turn left, where you will soon reach the car park.

6. Slaughters - The Slaughters Inn

Tel: 01451 822143 | Easy - 2 miles - 1hr 30min

This is a wonderful circular walk. You will pass through the delightful Upper and Lower Slaughters, where you will find the pub near the end of your walk. In between the villages there is wonderful scenery as you pass through pasture, and walk beside the River Eye. There may be livestock and there are quiet lanes and village roads. There is a stile with a gap for dogs.

How to get there – Upper and Lower Slaughters can be found between Stow-on-the-Wold and Bourton-on-the-Water, off the A429. Turn onto Copsehill Road, following the sign for Lower Slaughter. Continue through the village, staying on Copsehill Road. On the outskirts of the village you will see the layby on your left, opposite The Rectory.

Grid Reference – SP 16477228

Nearest Postcode – GL54 2HY

Parking – In a narrow layby on Copsehill Road, opposite The Rectory

Facilities – There are no facilities, except in the pub

You will need – Dog lead, dog bags

The Walk

❶ At the end of the layby you will see a fingerpost and a gate. Go through the gate and continue along the short path. There may be livestock, so keep your dog under close control or on a lead. You will reach and pass through another gate.

Continue straight ahead, beside the hedgerow and stock fence. You will begin to ascend gently to reach a stile. There is a gap for dogs beside the stile. Cross the stile and continue to another kissing gate. Pass through the kissing gate to reach a quiet road.

Turn left on this road. There is a neat stone wall on your right and a hedgerow on your left. Look out for the footpath sign on your left, which is about 100m along the road. On reaching it, pass through the gate and enter into a field. Keep your dog under close control or on a lead, as there may be livestock.

Turn right and continue on the worn path at the edge of the meadow. You will reach and pass through a gate in the hedgerow. Continue straight ahead, and cross another field. The field has four boundary hedgerows with mature standard trees. On reaching the corner of the field, pass through the gate. Continue straight ahead. When you see a farm gate on your right, pass through it, and reach a quiet road. Turn left and descend on the road. Immediately after passing a road on your right, cross the small green area and pass a bench, where you will reach a kissing gate. Pass through the kissing gate and continue straight

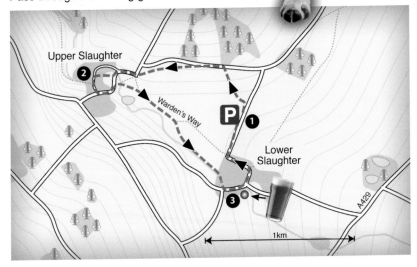

ahead, beside the stream on your left. You will reach and pass through another kissing gate. Turn left and cross the footbridge, beside the ford. ❷ Your dog can get water here. Continue to ascend on the quiet road through the picturesque village of Upper Slaughter.

Continue on the road, veering to your left and turn left on reaching the junction. Continue on the road for about 100m, and then turn right on reaching the fingerpost signed for Warden's Way. Pass beside the stone wall and hedgerow.

On reaching the end of the path, cross a footbridge over a stream. Your dog can get water here. Keep your dog under close control or on a lead and pass through a kissing gate into a field. Turn right on the worn path and ascend across the field, which has mature parkland trees.

On reaching a kissing gate, pass through it and cross the field ahead and slightly to your right on the worn path. At the end of the field pass through a gate and continue on the path between the fences. Pass alongside a river on your right, where your dog can cool down. At the end of the path you will reach a gate. Pass through the gate where you now walk between stone walls. Put your dog on a lead and pass through another gate and continue between stone walls, and houses. On reaching the road turn right. You are now in the idyllic village of Lower Slaughter.

You will pass a mill and craft shop and continue beside houses with the river on your right. As you turn a bend you will pass a footbridge and ford on your right. Ignore a fingerpost and footpath on your left and continue straight ahead. You will reach the main road. The pub is on your right. ❸

On leaving the pub, turn left on the main road and follow the Macmillan Way. Pass a church on your right and make use of the pavement. Continue on the road through the village, and ignore a footpath on your left on the edge of the village. Continue on the quiet road, there is no pavement for the last 200m. You will then reach back to your car.

7. Finstock - The Plough Inn

Tel: 01993 868333 Easy - 2.5 miles - 2hr

This is a lovely circular walk starting and ending at the pub. It is fairly level except for a short ascent on part of Dark Lane, which is a quiet byway. You will pass through quiet woodland and some forest plantation. There are no roads, except for a very short section on a quiet country lane. You will cross a meadow/pony paddock, and then continue through several large crop fields.

How to get there – From Oxford, take the A44 signed for Woodstock and Evesham. Turn left onto the B4437, signed for Charlbury. On reaching the village of Charlbury, turn left on Fawler Road (B4022), which is signposted for Finstock. On reaching Finstock village, turn left following the sign for Shops and Post Office, on School Road. Continue through the village until you reach a brown sign for The Plough Inn. Turn left, where on reaching a T-junction you will see the pub.

Grid Reference – SP 362161

Postcode – OX7 3BY

Facilities – There are no facilities, except in the pub

You will need – Dog lead, dog bags and water for your dog

The Walk

❶ With your back to the front of the pub, turn right on the road, and almost immediately turn left, on the byway known as Dark Lane. Continue between the gardens, and as you continue you will descend gently amongst the trees, with fields on either side.

Continue on this track for quite a distance (just over 1 mile), ignoring any footpaths and tracks on your left. You will pass through woodland and some forest plantations. Put your dog on a lead before you reach a large metal barn on your right. Continue straight ahead, where you will reach a road. **❷** Turn left on the road for about 20 yards, and then as the road levels take the footpath on your right.

There may be horses/ponies for the next section. Keep your dog under close control or on a lead and go through the kissing gate. Continue straight ahead. Cross a meadow and continue between the trees. You will pass a pheasant pen on your right, and as you leave the shade of the trees continue on the edge of the field, with the wood on your right.

Just before reaching the end of the field and immediately after you pass the horse shelter on your left, take a narrow path on your right. **❸**

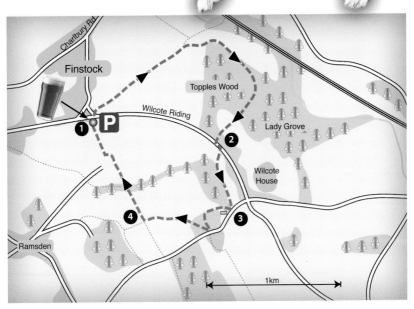

Cross a footbridge and then take a path on your left. Continue beneath the trees. When you leave the trees you will reach a large crop field. Turn left and continue on the edge of the field. Ignore the track on your left soon after.

Continue on the edge of the field, beside the fence line and woodland on your left. Pass a track on your left, which leads to two large barns. As you reach the corner of the field ignore two non-gated entrances into other fields, and then take the third entrance. Continue on the edge of the field with a hedgerow on your left. As you reach roughly halfway across the field, ignore the field entrance on your left in the gap in the hedge, and turn right. ❹ Continue beside the long grass/ditch on your left.

Continue beneath the power lines. On reaching the end of the field continue straight ahead between the trees, where you will reach another field. Continue straight ahead across the middle of the field. The power lines are now over on your left.

As the field ends on your right, continue straight ahead beside a hedgerow, remaining on the edge of the field on your left. On reaching the end of the field, pass through the gate and continue between stock fence and stone wall. At the end of the path put your dog on a lead and pass through the kissing gate. Continue straight ahead between the trees. You will soon reach the road, and the pub is on your right.

8. Birdlip - The Royal George Hotel

Tel: 01452 862506   Medium - 5.5 miles - 3hr 30min

This linear walk follows part of the Cotswold Way long distance route, for most of the walk, until you reach Birdlip. It is predominantly in woodland, where you will be on good forest tracks. The paths are undulating in places and there are some slightly steep ascents. You will pass a stream, where your dog can cool off. Horse riders and cyclists share the path. There is a quiet lane at the beginning of the walk and a busy road to cross in Birdlip. The pub is reached at the furthest point of your walk.

How to get there – From the M5 take the turn off at junction 11A, following the sign for London and Cirencester A417. Turn off the A417 when you see the sign for A46 Cheltenham and Stroud. At the roundabout turn right, following for Stroud. At the next roundabout continue straight ahead following for Stroud. Continue on this road for about 1 mile, and then turn left following the sign for Cooper's Hill. Continue on this road until you reach a 'No Through Road' sign. You will see the car park on your right.

Grid Reference – SO 891148
Postcode – GL3 4SB
Parking – Free in Cooper's Hill car park
Facilities – There are no facilities except in the pub
You will need – Dog lead, dog bags

The Walk

❶ From the car park go back to the road and turn right, following the sign on the fingerpost for the Cotswold Way (CW), which is a long distance footpath, and Birdlip. Continue to the end of the quiet road. You will have views in places on your left. ❷ At the end of the road continue straight ahead on the footpath, descending on the edge of woodland. There are some views on your left, where the trees allow.

When you pass the field on your left, you will continue through the middle of woodland. Just after an ascent, ignore the path on your right. Soon after, ignore a track on your right. On reaching a fingerpost, continue to follow the CW straight ahead, where another path will merge with the one you are on. On your left there is a stream, where your dog can get water in the small ravine. Sedges dominate the woodland floor in places.

Continue to follow the waymarkers for the CW, and ignore a track on your right. There are views in places, and you will see the lake of a trout farm in the distance. You will reach and continue beside a dilapidated stone wall on your left. On reaching another path, turn left and continue on the CW. You will reach and

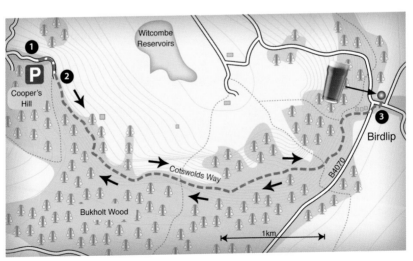

continue beside another stone wall on your left. A little further on you will reach another path, turn right (merge with the other path). Continue to follow the waymarker for the CW. Ignore a track on your left and continue straight ahead. You will pass a small parking bay (enough for two cars) on your left. Put your dog on a lead here, and continue straight ahead.

Continue past several houses, and on reaching a road cross to the other side and turn left. ❸ Ascend onto an elevated path beside the road. You will see the pub on the opposite side of the road just after. Cross the road and enter the pub at the side of the hotel.

On leaving the pub, cross the road and turn right. Continue on the elevated pavement. On reaching level with the road, cross to the other side and continue straight ahead, to retrace your steps following the CW waymarkers.

9. Buckholt Wood - The Black Horse Inn

Tel: 01452 812217   Medium - 3 miles - 2hr 30min

Buckholt Wood is on the edge of Cranham village. There are many paths, but the walk follows the waymarkers for the Cotswold Way long distance footpath for over half the way. The wood is dominated by beech trees in parts, and is mostly broadleaved trees. Paths can get muddy in places, where pendular sedge dominates the woodland floor. You will cross a stream, where your dog can get a drink, shortly before reaching the pub (which is three quarters of the way around). There are a couple of roads to cross, and a short distance of quiet lane through the village. There are no livestock, but there may be deer in the area.

How to get there – Cranham is just outside Gloucester. From the M5 turn off at junction 11A. Follow the sign for Cirencester on the A417. Turn off at the next exit, sign posted for Shurdington and Brockworth. At the roundabout turn right, following the sign for A46 Stroud. Continue on the A46 for just over 3 miles. Turn left, where you see the sign for Cranham, Scout Centre and Birdlip. Just after, turn right, following the sign for Cranham and Scout H.Q. The car park will be found on your left.

Grid Reference – SO 893 130   **Postcode** – GL4 8HP

Parking – Free in the car park on the edge of Cranham village

Facilities – There are no facilities, except in the pub

You will need – Dog lead, dog bags

Dog Friendly Pub Walks - Cotswolds

The Walk

① From the car park, take the path beside the vehicle barrier and then veer left on the worn path, following the waymarker for the Cotswold Way (CW). Ascend gently through the woodland, which is dominated by beech trees. Stay on this path, ignoring any paths to your left or right.

The ascent will become steeper as you continue. You will reach and continue between dead hedging. Keep your dog under close control as you leave the dead hedging, as there is a road ahead and there are no boundary fences. Another track merges with the one you are on. Put your dog on a lead, and ascend to a vehicle barrier. Pass beside the vehicle barrier and turn right. **②** Cross the road and continue on the path on the opposite side of the road, following the sign on the waymarker for CW.

Ascend into woodland. As you continue, ignore paths on your left and right and continue straight ahead. Continue on a main path where you will merge/turn right onto another main path, following the waymarker

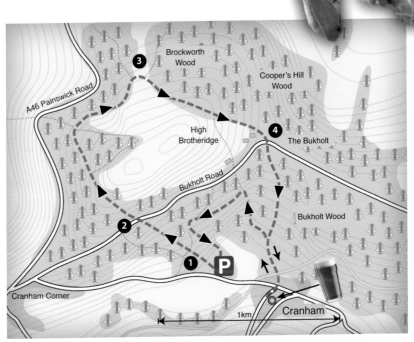

for the CW. Just after, you will begin to descend. Ignore a footpath on your right and continue to descend beside a stone wall on your left.

Soon after, on reaching a fork take the left path and descend a little more steeply. The woodland is now mixed broadleaved trees and hazel coppice. The path levels off as you reach a junction of paths. Ignore the first right path, and take the second right, which is waymarked for the CW. Continue straight ahead, on a fairly level path.

Pass a set of steps on your left, which lead to a road. Continue straight ahead, where you will ascend and descend beside the steeply sloped woodland on your left. There is a field beyond the trees on your right. Pass another waymarker and continue to follow the CW. You will leave the woodland edge and continue in an open area between the hedgerows. Take a footpath on your right, following the waymarker for the CW. Ascend the steps and ignore a path immediately on your right. Just after, on reaching another path, turn right. Pass through a kissing gate and continue to follow the CW, between hedges with fields beyond. ❸

On reaching the end of the fields, leave the path where it bends sharply to your left. Take a path on your right, which isn't marked. Ascend on the edge of the wood, with a field on your right. Pass through a gap in the post and

"*Where have our humans gone?*"

"They really can't be trusted off the lead!"

rail fence and continue straight ahead and ascend gradually amongst the beech trees on the edge of the wood. Ignore a path on your left and continue through the woodland ride (narrow grassland area).

On reaching another path and a wooden vehicle barrier, continue straight ahead, pass beside the barrier and descend through the wood. You will reach a track with a gate on your right. Put your dog on a lead, as there is a road ahead. Turn right and pass beside the gate. Pass beside an agricultural building on your right. On reaching another track turn left. ❹ On reaching the road, cross it and turn left. Take a footpath on your right shortly after. Descend into the wood, and just after cross a cycle track and continue straight ahead.

On reaching a fork take the path on your right. Continue to descend on a narrow path through mixed broadleaved wood, and ignore a path on your right. Pendular sedge dominates the ground flora. The path gets a little muddy on this section. Continue straight ahead, where a path will merge from your right. Ignore an ascending path on your left. On reaching another path, cross it and continue straight ahead. Descend on the path, where you will see houses on your right. Take a path on your right soon after. Descend to a stream, where your dog can get a drink. Put your dog on a lead, cross the stream via the stones and ascend gently between the houses.

On reaching the road, cross over and continue straight ahead, where you will reach the pub. On leaving the pub, turn right and retrace your steps. Cross the road and continue on the footpath between the houses. Cross the stream and ascend, turning left. Continue on the familiar path. Cross a path and continue straight ahead. Ignore the path from your outbound route, which veers to your right. Continue on the path straight ahead, where you will pass a white cycle stencil on the tree.

As you continue, keep your dog under close control and beware of cyclists. Soon you will ascend very steeply. The path will snake around the wooded hill. On reaching a narrow path turn left, where you now leave the cycle track. Continue on a level path. You will then descend quite steeply. Pass beside a field on your left and on reaching another path turn left. Ascend on the path and ignore a path on your right as you reach level ground. Continue straight ahead, where you will reach the car park.

"So what if I drink with a straw!"

10. Miserden - Carpenter's Arms

Tel: 01285 821283   Medium - 3.3 miles - 2hr

This circular walk starts and ends in the quiet village of Miserden. The walk passes through the estate grounds, on quiet tracks, over wooded hills and fields. There is a stream and a lake, where your dog can get a drink. You will leave the estate briefly on a quiet road, before taking the main entrance back into the estate beside the avenue of trees. There may be livestock grazing on parts of the walk, and there is a quiet road. The pub is located at the beginning/end of your walk.

How to get there – Miserden can be reached between Cirencester and Gloucester off the A417. Turn off the A417 when you see the sign for Syde, Winstone and Elkstone. Just after, turn left for Winstone. At the end of the road turn right, following the sign for Miserden. Continue to follow the signs for Miserden. You will reach the pub in the centre of the village.

Grid Reference – SO 938089   **Postcode** – GL6 7JA

Parking – In the pub car park (It is expected that if you use this car park you will be a customer in the pub)

Facilities – There are no facilities, except in the pub

You will need – Dog lead, dog bags

The Walk

❶ Pass the Carpenter's Arms pub on your left and then a sycamore tree, which has a seat built around it. On reaching the end of the road, pass through a kissing gate on your left. Keep your dog on a lead or under close control.

Descend on the sealed road. Pass a grand house on your far right. Continue through the estate grounds, with mature parkland trees and views of the wooded hillside and rolling hills. The path meanders down the hillside. You will reach a stone wall. Pass through a gateway and continue straight ahead, on the sealed path.

You will reach a stream on your right, where your dog can get a drink. You will reach a road on your right. Pass the road and continue straight ahead, ascending on the quiet access road. There is a wire fence and woodland on your right, and mature beech trees on your left.

As the road bends sharply to your left, turn off the road and continue straight ahead on the grass track, beside the fence. Pass a pheasant pen on your right. The track becomes sunken, where you will descend gently between banks. On reaching a gate, pass through it, and enter into a forest. You will reach a sealed track, where you turn left.

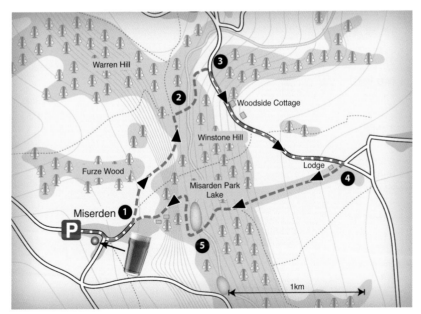

There is a woodland ride on your right, with a stream running through the middle, where your dog can get a drink. ❷ Cross a footbridge beside the ford, and continue to ascend on the sealed track. Continue in the valley, between wooded hills. Pass a track on your left and continue straight ahead, ascending gently.

The track becomes sunken as you ascend through the wood. As you leave the wood, put your dog on the lead. There are fields on both sides now. You will reach and pass through a gate and then reach a quiet road. ❸ Turn right on the road and ascend. You will pass a house on your left, and then pass a gate and a footpath on your right. Continue on the quiet road, which is now level.

Pass a footpath on your left. After some distance pass an old gatehouse on your right and then turn right, ❹ and pass through the wrought iron gates. Continue on the driveway, keeping your dog on a lead. As the driveway bends to your right and before you reach the stone gateposts, take the track on your left. Ignore the footpath on your left and continue straight ahead, following the blue waymarker. Descend on the grass track between trees.

The path becomes sunken as you descend on the wooded hillside. You will reach a lake. ❺ Continue past the lake on your right. Cross a footbridge and continue to a sealed track. Turn right on the track and continue beside the lake. Trees and scrub will block your view of the lake and you will ascend gradually. On reaching another sealed road, turn left. Continue to ascend and pass between old stone gateposts. There are mature cedars, and beyond the trees there are horse paddocks.

Ascend on the track, and you will soon pass the estate house on your left. Continue straight ahead, and on reaching the wrought iron gates pass through the smaller gate on your right. You will now be in a familiar spot. Continue straight ahead on the road through the village, where you will soon reach the pub.

11. Uley Bury - The Old Crown Inn

Tel: 01453 860502   Challenging - 2.5 miles - 2hr

Uley Bury is an Iron Age hill fort, dated around 300 B.C. It is a long, flat-topped hill just outside the village of Uley, near Dursley. The hill fort is reached near the beginning of the walk. There's an area beside the hill fort where you will have fantastic views on a clear day. There is a steep descent through broadleaved woodland, and then you will cross through farmland, before reaching the pub (just over halfway round). A steep ascent over pasture brings you back to the wood, where you will ascend back to the hill fort. There may be cattle for parts of the walk, and there is a quiet road in the village. There are a couple of stiles, but there are lift gates for your dog.

How to get there – From Stroud, take the B4066, signed for Selsley and Uley. Continue to follow the sign for Uley and Dursley. You will pass a brown sign for Uley Long Barrow, and then as you begin to pass a series of bends and descend, take the layby on your right.

Grid Reference – ST 786993

Postcode – GL11 5BH

Parking – Free in the layby

Facilities – In the pub

You will need – Dog lead, dog bags

The Walk

❶ From the parking bay, face the road and turn right. Take the footpath through the gate, and continue straight ahead between fences. On reaching an interpretation panel laid in stone, turn right. Continue on the narrow path between the fences and brambles, with the top section of the hill fort on your left beyond the fence. There is woodland on your right. Ignore a footpath with a stile on your right.

When you leave the woodland behind, the views on your right and ahead are fantastic. On reaching a gate straight ahead pass through it, and continue on the well-worn path, with views on your right. There may be cattle grazing. The hill fort slopes steeply on your right. Just before you go around a sharp left bend on the path, take a path on your right, which is signed Bridleway on a waymarker. **❷**

Descend between grass banks, which have many wild flowers in spring and summer. Cross a narrow path and continue to descend. You will reach a fence and gate with woodland beyond. Pass through the gate, where you can let your dog off the lead and descend quite steeply through the wood. On reaching a gate and stile, cross the stile, using the lift gate for your dog. Keep your dog under close control as there may be cattle/sheep in the field. Continue to descend on the edge of the field, beside a fence on your right. Continue on the tarmac track.

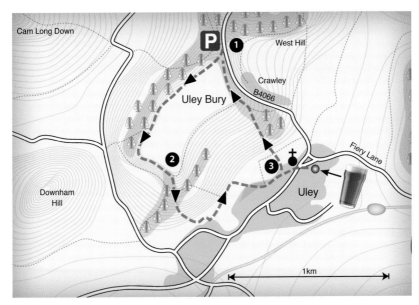

You will pass houses on your right. Ignore a kissing gate on your right, in the corner of the field and continue around the corner, staying on the edge of the field. Pass the houses on your right, and on reaching another field corner, go through the gate, and continue between the barbed wire fences. Ignore a stile on your left and right and continue on the path. Turn a corner, and continue beside the fences, with a hedgerow on your right and a field on your left.

Pass through a kissing gate and continue on the edge of a field, beside gardens on your right. In the corner of the field, go through a kissing gate, ignore a footpath on your left and cross a track. Take the footpath on the opposite side. Ascend gently between hedgerows. As you reach the cemetery on your right, put your dog on a lead, as there is a road ahead. Continue on the path, pass the church, and on reaching the road cross it. Turn left, where you will reach the pub.

On leaving the pub, retrace your steps on the footpath beside the church. Just before you reach the end of the cemetery, take the footpath on your right. **3** Ascend gently between the hedgerows. On reaching a kissing gate, put your dog on a lead or under close control and enter into the field. Continue straight ahead, ascending steeply through the middle of the sloped field towards woodland. On reaching the stock fence beside the wood, turn left.

Continue on the edge of the field beside the wood on your right. You will reach and continue on a worn path. Pass through a gate and enter into the wood. Continue on the worn path ahead, and slightly to your left. Ascend steeply through the woodland. At the end of the path on reaching the woodland edge, go through a gate. Keep your dog under close control as there may be cattle. Continue straight ahead, where you will reach and continue beside a stock fence on your right. There is a bramble bank on your left. As you reach grass hillocks, the gradient will steepen. At the top of the hill there are views on your right. The plateau of the hill fort is on your left. On reaching the end of the hill fort go through a gate and turn right. You are now on a familiar path. Retrace your steps back to the parking bay. Remember there is a busy road ahead. Keep your dog under close control.

12. Tyndale Monument - The Black Hors

Tel: 01453 543777   Med/Chall - 2.5 miles - 2hr 30min

This circular walk ascends through wonderful broadleaved woodland, where there are many mature beech trees. At the top of the hill you will reach a wonderful floristic meadow, where the monument stands. The Tyndale Monument was erected in 1866 in remembrance of William Tyndale, who was the first to translate the bible into English, and as a consequence was later killed. Take some change as the monument is open and there is an honesty box for donations. You can climb the 120 steps, where on a clear day you will be rewarded with fantastic views.

How to get there – The walk is in North Nibley, and can be approached from the A38, between Gloucester and Bristol, and close to Newport. Turn off the A38 when you see the sign for Upper Wick and Lower Wick. Shortly after you pass under a road bridge turn left, following the sign for North Nibley. On reaching a green triangle turn left, following the sign for Wotton-Under-Edge and Dursley. At the end of the road turn right, and follow the sign for North Nibley. Continue through the village, and at the end of the road, cross the main road, and continue straight ahead, where you will find the pub on your left and the car park a little further up the road.

Grid Reference – ST 741958   **Postcode** – GL11 6DT
Parking – The pub car park (if using the pub car park, it's expected that you will be a paying customer in the pub).
Facilities – At the pub
You will need – Dog lead, dog bags

The Walk

❶ From the pub car park, go to the head of Barrs Lane, next to the pub. Cross the road and turn left, following the road sign for Chipping Sodbury. After about 100 yards cross the road and continue on the Cotswold Way (CW), which is a long-distance footpath, signed for Tyndale Monument. This path is also a bridleway, so you may pass horse riders.

Ascend on the path, which can be quite steep in places, between wooded banks. Soon after, ignore a footpath on your right. Take the next footpath on your right, where you remain on the CW. Ascend steeply for a short section, amongst the trees.   After you pass a waymarker, keep to your left. You will soon ascend out of the wood. Turn right, and continue on the edge of the meadow, towards the monument. **❷**

You can enter the monument and climb the 120 steps. On leaving the monument, with your back to the entrance take the path ahead and to your right. Continue on the edge of the meadow, where you can enjoy amazing views on your right. You will pass a topograph on your right, and then continue near to a stock fence over on your right.

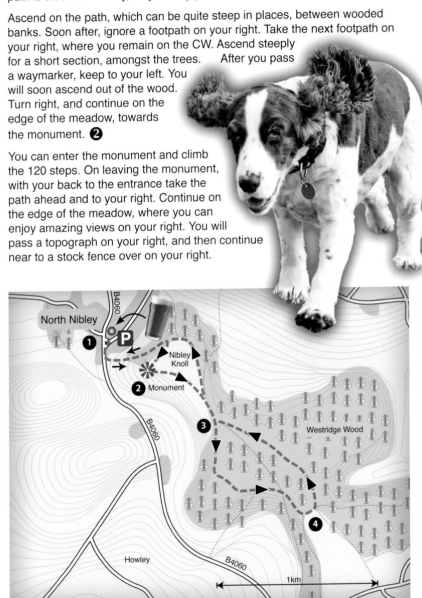

At the end of the meadow take the path straight ahead, where you will enter back into woodland. Pass beside a stone slab and a gate. Just after, turn right, leaving the bridleway. ❸ Ignore a path on your left and continue straight ahead. Shortly afterwards ignore a path on your right and continue on the CW.

Ascend gradually, and after the path levels off you will reach a junction of paths. Take the second left. On reaching another path, turn left. Stay on the main path, ignoring any minor paths. Follow the waymarkers for the CW. On reaching another path, on the edge of the wood turn left. You have now left the CW.

Continue on the edge of the wood, with a field beyond some trees on your right. You will reach paths left and right. ❹ Take the path on your left. As you continue there is coppiced hazel on your right. On reaching a fork, take the path on your right. Ignore a path on your left, and then turn a sharp right. Almost immediately after, you will reach another fork. Take the path on your left.

On reaching another path turn left. Continue on the main path, ignoring any minor paths on your left and right. There is hazel coppice on both sides of the path. After some distance, ignore a left and right turn and continue straight ahead. You will merge onto another path and then begin to descend. Ignore a path on your left, which backtracks, and then take the path on your right.

Continue to descend. You will soon reach several paths. Continue straight ahead, on a familiar path. Pass between the concrete slab and gate. You will soon reach back to the meadow. Take the path straight ahead, through the middle of the meadow. At the end of the meadow, continue straight ahead, and enter into the wood. Stay on the main path. Ignore a path on your left and descend. You will pass beside a gate on your left. Ignore a path on your left, which is marked CW. You will now continue to descend on a familiar path, where you will retrace your steps back to the car park. Remember there is a busy road ahead, so as you pass a path on your left put your dog on a lead. On reaching the main road, turn right, where you will soon reach the pub.

13. Swineford - The Swan

Tel: 0117 9323101   Easy - 4.5 miles - 2hr 30min

The circular walk starts off beside a crop field. You will briefly pass through the village of Upton Cheyney, and then continue through farmland on part of the Monarch's Way long distance footpath. You will then join the River Avon Trail, which is another long-distance path, beside the river. There may be livestock grazing for parts of the walk, but a lot of the farmland is arable. You will cross a busy road at the end of your walk, before reaching the pub. Although you will be beside the river, the sides are steep and there is very little access for your dog.

Please Note – There is a squeeze stile, therefore any breed larger than a Labrador may not get through.

How to get there – This walk is located on edge of the Cotswolds, between Bath and Bristol, off the A431. On reaching Swineford, follow the brown sign for the car park and picnic area, which is at the side of the Swan pub.

Grid Reference – ST 690692   **Postcode** – BS30 6LN

Parking – Free in the car park

Facilities – There are no facilities except in the pub

You will need – Dog lead, dog bags

The Walk

❶ From the car park, go back towards the exit to your parking bay and turn left. Pass beside the vehicle barrier and continue between the bollards for about 10 yards. Turn left and cross the grass to reach the kissing gate. Go through the kissing gate and turn right. Keep your dog on the path, to avoid crop damage. Continue on the edge of the field, beside the hedgerow on your right.

At the end of the field go through the kissing gate, cross a sleeper bridge and continue between a stock fence and hedgerow. Ascend gently to begin with, and as you continue the gradient steepens. Go through another kissing gate and continue to ascend between the hedgerow and stock fence on the grass path.

Just before reaching a gate ahead, turn left and go through another kissing gate. Continue on the narrow path, between the stock fence and hedgerow. On reaching a red brick wall, keep your dog under close control or on a lead. Continue on the path, where you will reach a gate and a road. Cross the road, pass a bench and go through the kissing gate, keeping your dog on a lead or under close control as there may be livestock or horses.

On reaching the corner of a field, turn right and continue on the worn path near the edge of the field. As the fence line/hedgerow veers to your right, cross to the other side of the field and turn left. Now continue beside the fence on your right. You are now on the Monarch's Way, which is a long-distance path. At the end of the field, ignore the kissing gate on your right and continue

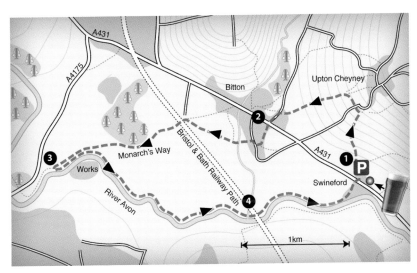

straight ahead, where you pass through the squeeze stile.

Descend on a concrete path. Go between the gap, crossing over the bar, and continue between the fence and hedgerow. At the end of the path go through the kissing gate and continue on the field edge, with a post and rail fence on your right. You will reach and pass through another kissing gate. Cross the field diagonally to your left, on the worn grass path and head towards the houses. You will see a kissing gate in the corner of the field. Put your dog on a lead and pass through the kissing gate.

Continue between gardens, where you will reach a road. Turn left and continue, where you will reach a main road. ❷ Cross the main road and then enter Church Lane. At the end of the lane, enter the churchyard. After roughly 20 yards turn right. Leave the churchyard via a kissing gate, and then turn right on the quiet road. Soon after, turn left where you see the footpath marker. Pass between the stone post and then go through the gate. Continue on a raised path, beside a driveway. You will join the driveway, where you will pass a pumping station on your left. Continue straight ahead and cross a concrete bridge. Pass a stile on your left and shortly after turn right, just as you reach a concrete slope and go through the kissing gate. Continue on the edge of the horse paddocks with a hedgerow on your right. Pass through a kissing gate and continue on the edge of the field.

Turn around a corner of the field, ignoring the stone stile, following the sign on the fingerpost for Keynsham. On reaching another field corner, put your dog on a lead and pass through the kissing gate. Turn left on the quiet road, and pass under a disused railway bridge. At the end of the road go through

two gates and enter into another field. Keep your dog under close control or on a lead. Turn right and continue on the edge of the field, with a stock fence on your right.

On reaching the corner of the field, pass through the gate, cross the sleeper bridge and go through another gate. Turn left and head towards a derelict chapel. Pass the chapel on your left, and then veer to your left across the field. Go through the kissing gate, cross a sleeper bridge and continue straight ahead. Go through another kissing gate on your left at the end of the path. Turn right, and continue on the edge of another field, beside the hedgerow on your right.

At the end of the field, go through a kissing gate and continue on the edge of another field. On reaching the end of the field, pass through a gate and continue straight ahead, crossing over a field. Pass a stone barn over on your right. Pass another small barn on your right, and then one on your left. Pass Avondale House on your right. Continue on the tarmac path across the field.

When you reach a stone tower with a pipe line across the river, go to the tower and turn left. ❸ Continue on a grass path, which backtracks, now beside the River Avon, and following the Avon Trail. Take care that your dog doesn't go in the river, as the banks are steep. You will pass an industrial section of the river on the opposite side. Continue beside the river for quite a distance, passing through many kissing gates, on the edge of many fields. Eventually you will cross a bridge. Keep your dog under close control or on a lead as there is a drop ahead. Continue straight ahead, where you will cross a grass area and then cross a tarmac path.

Continue beside the river, where you will pass under a disused railway bridge. ❹ The drop into the water is on your right. Pass through a kissing gate, and then continue as before, on the edge of fields, beside the river on your right. When you see the Swan pub ahead of you, put your dog on a lead, as there is a road ahead. Pass through the kissing gate, cross the road and enter into the pub. On leaving the pub, go to the beer garden and exit out of the car park. Turn right on the access road, pass through a gate beside the cattle grid and continue where you will reach back to the car park.

"It's been a hard day's night and I've been working like a dog!"

14. River Avon - The Boathouse

Tel: 01225 482584   Easy - 5 miles - 3hr

This linear walk follows beside the River Avon for the entire time. There are lots of trees beside the river, and areas where your dog can access the water. You will also walk beside a meadow and an arable field. The river is popular with race boats, so beware if your dog likes to swim in the water, as the boats are fast and rowed backwards, therefore your dog won't be seen. You will walk close to a railway for a short section of the walk. There is a short section beside a busy road, and the pavement is narrow as you cross over the bridge. The pub, which is also beside the river, is at the furthest point of your walk.

How to get there – This walk starts in Saltford Village, which is on the outskirts of Bath. Take the A36 (which becomes A4) from Bath, in the direction of Bristol. When you reach Saltford Village take the first road on your right, which is narrow. Go under the railway bridge and continue on the road. You will reach the car park further along on your left.

Grid Reference – ST 687673   **Postcode** – BS31 3EX

Parking – Free in the car park

Facilities – Toilets in the car park (small charge)

You will need – Dog lead, dog bags

The Walk

❶ Keep your dog on a lead to begin with. From the car park, turn right on the road, and continue beside the River Avon on your left. Pass the houses on your right, and you will also pass Saltford Brass Mill on your left,   which is a scheduled ancient monument. Soon after, take a footpath on your left. Descend the steps and continue on a path, which leads to a weir.

You will pass The Riverside pub on your right, and continue on the tarmac path. Ascend the concrete steps and cross a bridge over an inlet. Continue straight ahead, beside the river. You will pass a rowing club on your right and then you will pass through a kissing gate. **❷** Continue between the hedgerows, where you will soon reach and continue close to a railway line on your right. There is a stock fence, which will keep your dog away from the line.

Pass through another kissing gate, and continue beneath the trees, beside the river. After some distance, ignore a footpath on your right. You will pass a low stone wall, with a river inlet on your right. Just after this, the railway line will veer off on your right. The area opens up, as you continue beside a meadow/crop field on your right. You will see a large house on your left in the distance on top of the hill. This is Dean Hill house.

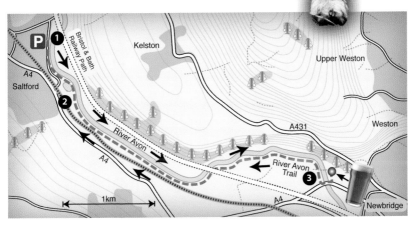

76

You will pass under a disused railway bridge. Ignore a path on your right immediately after. Continue beside the river. Veer to your left as you reach a copse of trees. As you leave the canopy of the trees, turn left on the concrete path and head towards the arched road bridge. ❸ Put your dog on the lead before reaching the bridge. Just before you reach the bridge, leave the concrete path and take a path on your left. Ascend to the road and turn left on the narrow pavement. Immediately after you cross the bridge, take the footpath on your left. Descend to the arch of the bridge and turn right. Cross the pub car park, where you will reach the pub.

On leaving the pub, retrace your steps back across the bridge, and then along the river. Remember once you reach the weir, to take the footpath on your left just after. Turn right on reaching the road, and continue to the car park.

15. Combe Hay - The Wheatsheaf

Tel: 01225 833504   Challenging - 3 miles - 2hr 30min

This is a wonderful walk, starting in the very pretty village of South Stoke. There are wonderful views soon after you start your walk. Much of the walk is on tracks, between fences and farmland. At the halfway point you will reach the pub in the village of Combe Hay. There is some meadows and farmland, where you may be amongst livestock. There is an ascent through woodland and a hay field shortly before the end of the walk. You will cross a small stream, where your dog can get water.

How to get there – South Stoke is just outside Bath. Head south, on the A367. Turn left on the B3110, following the sign for Frome, Hinton, Charterhouse and Midford. Continue through part of Midford on the B3110, and turn right at the Cross Keys Pub, following the sign for South Stoke. At the end of the lane you will reach South Stoke.

Grid Reference – ST 746612   **Postcode** - BA2 7DX

Parking – On the roadside in South Stoke village (please park considerately)

Facilities – There are no facilities, except in the pub

You will need – Dog lead, dog bags

The Walk

❶ The walk starts at the entrance to the church. At the end of the road, take the footpath to the right of an entrance to the kissing gate and follow the footpath on a track, beside Manor Farm, which is on your left. On reaching a concrete track turn right. Manor Farm. Go through sign. Continue

Continue to ascend, where you will have wonderful views on your left. On reaching the top of the hill, you can stop at a viewpoint on your left. There is a bench behind the stone wall. Continue straight ahead on the track. Ignore a couple of paths on your right, in the gap in the stone wall and continue straight ahead. Continue between the trees on the path, and ignore a track which veers to your right. You will reach and pass through a kissing gate. Keep your dog on a lead or under close control and continue on the edge of a crop field, with a stock fence on your left. As you reach close to the corner of the field, put your dog on a

lead. You will reach and pass through a kissing gate. Turn immediately left onto another track (not onto the road). ❷ Ignore a footpath on your right, and descend on the tarmac track through woodland, with a stock fence on your left. This is a byway, therefore listen for traffic and keep your dog under close control.

Continue straight ahead, where the byway bends sharply to your right. After a short distance you will begin to ascend quite steeply. Shortly after you will descend again. Leave the cover of trees, and continue on the track between fences, with horse paddocks beyond. Keep your dog under close control, and on reaching a brick wall put your dog on a lead. Continue between the walls, and pass a house on your left. Continue on the quiet road. You will pass a small cemetery on your right. Ignore a footpath on your right, and continue to descend on the road. ❸ Just before the end of the road you will reach the pub on your left.

Leave the pub at the entrance to the car park and turn left on the quiet road. Shortly after, on reaching another road, turn left. Ascend on the quiet road, where you will have views into the valley on your right. As you continue, ascend on the 'No Through' road on your left.

When you reach the entrance to Caisson House veer to your left. Continue straight ahead, and pass beside the houses on your right. After you have passed the houses continue between hedgerows on a track. You will pass Ravley Farm stables on your left. Continue straight ahead, between the trees. As you continue, you will pass beside sloping fields on your left beyond the fence, with a hedgerow on your right.

Ascend gently to a gate. Don't go through the gate but turn right, following the waymarker for the Limestone Link. Descend and go through a kissing

"Only well behaved humans allowed!"

gate. Keep your dog on the path, as there may be ground-nesting birds. Ignore a path on your right and continue straight ahead on the well-worn path, through a wonderful floristic meadow.

At the end of the meadow, go through the kissing gate and descend between the trees. Continue to descend through another meadow. On reaching a fingerpost enter into woodland, cross a stream, where your dog can get a drink, and then turn left. Shortly after, you will reach another sloping meadow. Ascend on the obvious path. On reaching the end of the field, go through a kissing gate, cross a track and continue straight ahead, beside a stock fence on your left. There are terraced cottages on your left.

Continue to ascend in the wood, between barbed wire fences. You will reach a gate. Pass through a squeeze stile on your left. For large breeds of dog, there is a large gap to the right of the gate. Continue straight ahead, between the hedgerows, with fields beyond.

On reaching a field, continue on the obvious worn path, which ascends, and cuts across the field horizontally to your left. Keep your dog under close control in case of livestock, and there is a road ahead. On reaching the corner of the field, go through a squeeze stile and turn left onto the quiet road. Ascend for a short distance. Pass two concrete tracks on your left and continue straight ahead. You will now be on a familiar path. Retrace your steps back to South Stoke village, where you have parked your car.

Dog Friendly Pub Walks - Cotswolds

'We are the working girls with natural curls!'

16. Avoncliff - Cross Guns

Tel: 01225 862335   Medium - 2 miles - 1hr 30min

This circular walk begins at the aqueduct on the Avon Canal towpath. After walking along the canal, you will cross the canal and pass through meadows, where you will reach a wonderful quiet broadleaved woodland. You will ascend gently on an undulating path. There is a short section on a quiet country lane, where you will reach the pub and the canal near the end of the walk.

How to get there – Avoncliff is just outside Bradford-on-Avon and Winsley. From Bradford-on-Avon, continue in the direction of Bath on Belcombe Road. Shortly after leaving the town, turn left, where you see the sign for Avoncliff Train Station. At the end of the road, you will reach the car park.

Grid Reference – ST 804600

Nearest Postcode – BA15 1LZ

Parking – Free in the car park, beside the train station

Facilities – In the pub

You will need – Dog leads, dog bags and water for your dog

The Walk

❶ Keep your dog on a lead to begin this walk. From the car park, face the canal and turn left. Cross the railway bridge and the aqueduct. Continue straight ahead on the canal towpath. Your dog can be off lead now, but under close control as cyclists use the towpath. Ignore a footpath on your left, which is signed to Barton Farm, and continue beside the canal.

❷ On reaching a wooden bridge (173) cross it, turn right and continue beside the canal on your right. Cross a footbridge and go through a kissing gate. Put your dog on a lead or under close control, as there may be livestock. Continue on the edge of the field, with a post and rail fence on your right.

On reaching the end of the field, go through another kissing gate and continue straight ahead, but slightly to your left. Ascend gently through

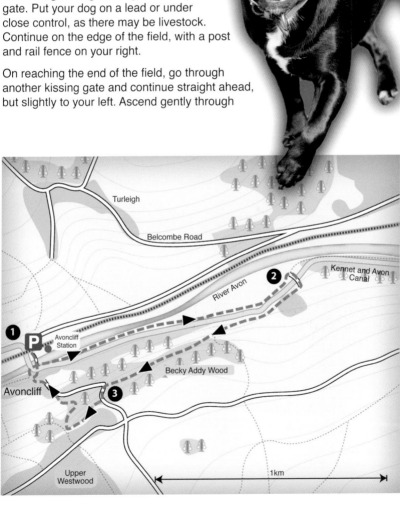

the field on the worn grass path. On reaching the opposite side of the field, pass through another kissing gate. Continue on an undulating path on the edge of woodland.

Ignore any minor paths, and continue straight ahead on the obvious path. After a while you will continue deeper into the wood, leaving the woodland edge. Keep your dog under close control, as there is a quiet road ahead. ❸ On reaching the road turn left and ascend quite steeply for a short distance.

On reaching a sharp left bend in the road, take the path on your right. Ignore a footpath on your left and continue straight ahead on an access road, where you will pass several houses. Continue straight ahead on a narrow path between gardens. Immediately before you reach a road, turn right. Ignore a path on your left almost immediately and continue straight ahead between hedgerows. Pass under a footbridge, ignore a footpath on your left and continue straight ahead, descending on the edge of a wood. There are fields beyond the fence on your left.

You will reach and continue beside a stone wall on your right. On reaching a gate, put your dog on a lead, go through the gate and cross a track. Continue straight ahead, where you will reach a quiet road. Turn left and descend on the quiet road. You will pass a car park on your left. Descend the steps on your right and keep your dog on a lead. Turn right, and continue beside a stone wall on your left, with the River Avon beyond it. Turn right and ascend, where you will have views on your left to the river. You will reach the pub at the top of the path.

On leaving the pub, keep your dog on a lead; ascend on the path straight ahead and to your left. At the top of the path turn right and cross the aqueduct and the railway bridge once again, where you will reach back to your car.

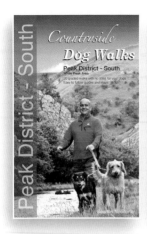

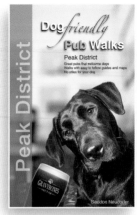

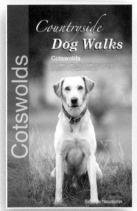

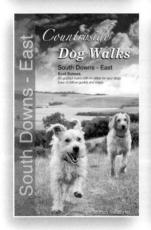

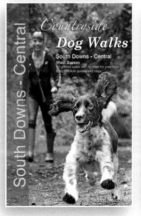

www.countrysidedogwalks.co.uk

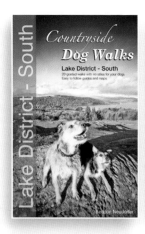

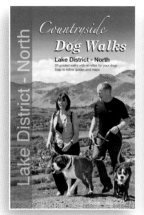

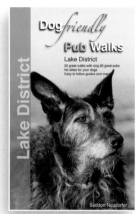

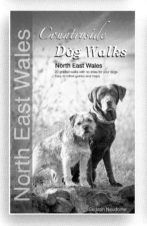

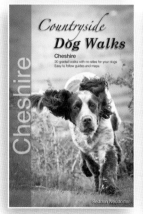

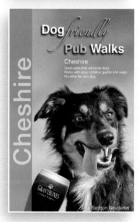

Home Made Dog Treats
Recipe Book

Seddon Neudorfer

New Release Nov - 2016

Simple recipes made from ingredients in your kitchen

Healthy ingredients to ensure a healthy dog

Fun and easy to make

Wet Nose
Publishing Ltd

"Cooking treats is easy"